OF SOME IMI

CW01572483

Also by Joy Howard

From Grey Hen Press
SECOND BITE
(with Hilary J Murray and Gina Shaw)
EXIT MOONSHINE

Edited by Joy Howard from Grey Hen Press
A TWIST OF MALICE
CRACKING ON
NO SPACE BUT THEIR OWN
GET ME OUT OF HERE!
THE PRICE OF GOLD
RUNNING BEFORE THE WIND
TRANSITIONS
OUTLOOK VARIABLE
SHADES OF MEANING
EXTRAORDINARY FORMS
SONGS FOR THE UNSUNG
VASTER THAN EMPIRES
FURTHER THAN IT LOOKS
OUT OF CONTEXT
MEASURING THE DEPTH
REFLECTED LIGHT

From Ward Wood Publishing
REFURBISHMENT
From Arachne Press
FORAGING

OF SOME IMPORTANCE

A Celebration

Edited by Joy Howard

First published in 2020 by Grey Hen Press
PO Box 269
Kendal
Cumbria
LA9 9FE
www.greyhenpress.com

ISBN   978-1-9996903-7-3

Printed by Flexpress, Birstall, Leicester LE4 3BY

Good women have limited views of life, their horizon is so small, their interests are so petty.

Oscar Wilde: *A Woman of No Importance*

Contents

Preface

Half the Human Race

Say we have tiny, dainty feet that fit,
that tiptoe over broken glass or gravel paths
or decorated egg-shells. Say our ankles are
well-turned, our heels are weapon-sharp.
Say our knees are shocking. Say

our nature's pairing, braising, managing
small things. Say we slapped our clothes
on river stones, we mangled, bleached
and starched, breathed steam and saved
the ends of soap against the shortages. Say

we're sweethearts, dolls with waists and hips
that cannot hold our vital organs, say we're
posable, blow-up generous, bonny, plus-size.
Say nice arse, a lovely pair. Say skin like silk,
like leather; say damaged by the sun. Then say

we're clavicle and fingernail, elbow, nape
and lobe. Say we're tearful. Say we're all
of this and none of it and more, and this
is nothing like the end of it. Say.

Susan Utting

The Women

The Survivor

A woman sits in a corner of sun
tracing a poem. Slowly
she is woven into it like the day
as smells of burning
carry her outside.

There, soldiers and jailers
are blocking the street:
books are being burnt –
thousands of words collapsing
in on each other. Suddenly
she sees her own fate:
her fellow-poet is taken
leaving her only silence.

She goes back to continue the poem:
it will go on for twenty years
islanded in her head
and Russia will remember her
as a lover
waiting for the ice-walls to break,
for her hermit's cry
to be carried like fire
from hand to hand.

Katherine Gallagher

Anna Akhmatova (1889–1966)

15

How Strange We Are

The rock spires whooped, snow whipped
at skin and Henriette d'Angeville
wished for cucumber facecream. When her guides offered ladders
and hands to help her, she refused. Instead pressed
her small feet to the brink of glaciers,
was resolute above crevasses.

Stood pin-neat in the whiteness, feet like a dancer's,
in her own design of pantaloons in Scottish tartan tweed.
Below them, silk stockings, and red flannel underwear next to the skin.
The pantaloons were lined with fleece, and were, she feared,
un peu coquette; so over it all she wore a dress,
same tartan, firmly belted.

Henriette – unmarried in the snows, and forty-four –
packed a bone shoehorn, because
it was not strictly needed. In rare ice brilliance she squinted
through green goggles. She burned with thirst.
She waited weeks for the weather to clear
and recorded the catches in her heart,
the wildness of her passion
for the mountain.

Nauseous, pulse hammering, she made her guides promise
to carry her body to the top, if she died.
She cut *Vouloir c'est pouvoir* into summit ice, they hoisted her
into the dark blue sky and shouted
'You are higher than Mont Blanc!'
and she opened her hands to her icy lover
tumbled a pigeon into the wind.
La curieuse chose que nous she wrote later
in her green notebook.

Jean Atkin

Henriette d'Angeville (1794–1871)

16

Showbiz

She is better than an actress, she's a woman. Victor Hugo

I was twenty. She was La Divina.
I could handle a cheetah, monkeys, owls,

her six chameleons but when she came home
with a lion on a leash our marriage was over.

The papers delight. The tours, her extravaganzas,
the son whose debts she pays off, always in cash.

The knee injury as Floria Tosca. For years
refusing crutches, wheelchairs, artificial legs.

Instead, getting herself carried round in a Louis XV-
styled palanquin until amputation became inevitable.

Mesmerizing audiences worldwide despite
language divides. A satin-lined coffin to sleep in,

rehearse her gestures and voice or study
Salome, that play Oscar specially wrote for her.

She detests knowing in advance, she said,
what her Chef serves for dinner but hundred

thousand times more what – for better or worse –
will happen to her. Her weird passion for death

scenes. Outdoing Cleopatra and her venomous asp
with two garter snakes. Ever eccentric, my Divina.

Elsa Fischer

Sarah Bernhardt (1844–1923)

17

Song Book

for Sylvia Miles

Maid of honours, her book has forty-two songs
writ in an English hand, but not her final singing.
O Death rock me asleep

I will give you pleasure dear sang Ann
perhaps to more than one man, perhaps not.
O Death rock me asleep

Mistresse A Bolleyne loved de Sermisy
and Josquin, love songs and prayers.
O Death rock me asleep

Flirt's scrapbook for singing the hours
or a scholar's Missa plurium modulorum?
O Death rock me asleep

Lute and harp, falcon and pomegranate.
Jouyssance vous donneray, she sang.
O Death rock me asleep

Penelope Shuttle

Ann Boleyn (1501–1536)

18

Self Portrait as a Palette

Here is Maman at my shoulder, cutting my hair short
as I asked. There is Papa: the atelier and
the mansions he gave me but never stayed to share.

Here are the years of happiness. Spring sky.
Hope of that first kiss, rustle of branches,
grasses, skirts. A blackbird's camera eye.

Here clenched under my nails, the morass:
storm clouds, forest. Brown stuff seams ripped up and re-sewn.

Here as if chanced on – poised as the single brushstroke tree
in the background but fought for, hunted: the heart, hart, art:
my humbling, noble prey.

Here limelight. Status. Medals. Acclaim.
Below, blood of the abattoir mixed with mine.
Oncoming night. With which I wrestle
to flush out and flesh out all my creatures
great and small.

Julia Deakin

Rosa Bonheur (1822–1899)

A Song at Imbolc

Now at spring's wakening, short days are lengthening and after St. Bridget's Day,
I'll raise my sail. Antoine Ó Raifteiri

A blind man, on a stone bridge in Galway
or the road to Loughrea, felt the suns's rays
in his bones again and praised the sycamore and oak,
crops still drowsy in the seed, wheat, flax and oats.
His song rising, he praised Achill's eagle, Erne's hawk
and in beloved Mayo, young lambs, kids, foals,
and little babies turning towards birth.

Blind Raftery invoked Bridget, Ceres of the North,
born into slavery at Faughert, near Dundalk
to an Irish chieftain and a foreign slave.
Why, of all small girls in so distant a century born
is she honoured, still, in place-names, constant wells,
new rushes plaited to protect hearth, home and herd?

Bridget, goddess, druidess of oak, or saint – a girl
who gifted her father's sword to a beggar for bread,
we, who have wounded the engendering seas and earth,
beg you to teach us again, before it grows too late,
your neglected, painstaking arts of nurture and of care.

Moya Cannon

St Bridget of Kildare (c 451–525)

20

In St Martin's Place

Erect, slender, keen faced,
you stand, poised for nursing,
a matron's cap on your head, bow under the chin,
alone on your high plinth,
part of your monument made of Cornish granite,
protecting you this Sunday afternoon.

One statue amongst others, national buildings
rising out the Charing Cross Road,
you – *woman, spinster, commoner* – are equal
to the National Portrait Gallery: to your right;
Nelson on his column, in front, flanked by regal lions;
to your left, by St Martin in the Fields, its Anglican presence.

Caught up in World War 1, it is said
you did not set off to be a martyr –
but qualities you had – the qualities
carved into the stone on which you stand –
Humanity, Fortitude, Devotion and Sacrifice:
gave you that thread, what is called Belief.

Sara Boyes

Edith Cavell (1865–1915)

21

Beyond Light

That the light that shone through tall windows
onto distillation flasks and filters
could be part of something more,
could see through the skin on her cracked hands,
was a beacon in the long hours.

That she asked for her wedding dress to be dark blue
and of thick material to serve for work
was typically practical,
that later on the long sleeves covered her bruises
was an unexpected benefit.

That she could crush and grind a tonne of grey ore
wash and boil it with acid and carbonate,
filter it to a pinch of white salt that could hardly
be seen or weighed but was the undoing of atoms,
fuelled her exhaustion.

That the test tube she carried in her pocket
glowed with a faint light was an intriguing discovery,
that she took the discovery home
on her clothes, in her hands,
traced its code in the ink as she wrote,
recorded it in the pages of her cookery book –
revealed itself as slowly as the ghosts
on the x-rays she developed.

Ilse Pedler

Marie Curie (1867–1934)

1913

It was the centenary of the births
of David Livingstone and Wagner,
Oxford won the boat race.
There was a coup d'état in Turkey,
a great fire in Tokyo. The stolen
Mona Lisa was retrieved in Florence.

The Panama Canal was opened.
a Dowager Empress died,
a Queen, the inventor, Mr Diesel.
Ships were launched, treaties signed,
Aston Villa won the cup.

And sometime in early June
a young woman bought
two violet, white and green flags,
and a ticket for a ball on the evening
of the 4th – items listed that day
amongst her belongings, together with
a race card and return stub of her ticket.

Margaret Beston

Emily Wilding Davison (1872–1913)

Flowers for the Dog Days

hydrangeas show a dusty parchment pink

    stilt-walking sunflowers peer over walls

phlox and dahlia hurl out fairground music

    fading fuchsia blood-stains pavements

chrysanthemums warn of chill to come

    of leaves now readying for fall and rot

and a sea of unseasonal cellophane washes up

    outside a palace gate

Joy Howard

Diana, Princess of Wales (1961–1997)

24

Flight Plan

'I more or less mortgaged the future. Without regret, however, for what are futures for?'

Even as you were honing a desire
for the horizon and beyond
in an old abandoned carriage
behind your childhood home

journeying across maps
tasting names of destinations
rolling their strange consonants
around your mouth

Timbuctu   Ngami   Khartoum

the stars were shifting –
aligning to set your course
over the loneliest stretches
and out into the sunline

Fortaleza   Dakar   Karachi

nothing – not even your belly-sledge
escapades – further and faster –
racing into a future you mortgaged
with such aplomb

prepared you for the signals
that echoed into nothing
how the atmosphere absorbed
your voice – your position in the world

Akyab   Singapore   Lae

how they called for you
searched for you over generations
how your final flight plan
would leave you *alone with the stars*

Deborah Sloan

Amelia Earhart (1897–?)

25

Miniature

Nicholas Hilliard (1605–1609)

In painting me, the limner does enhance
himself, though not by much. One royal brat
the less or more for his portfolio
makes little odds when queens and kings and heads
of state have been his stock in trade. My face
is not more beautiful than theirs, my dress
displays no jewels, is not at fashion's height.
More hoyden than my brothers, I have tamed
my hair to something less than lion's mane
for him. This portrait will be touted round
the courts of Europe to ensnare my mate.

There is no hint of what I will become:
a scholar, poet, queen of snowbound lands
I barely see, thanks to my father's perfidy,
and not of this. Yet I, and not my brothers,
will prevail. A century from now my own grandson
ascends the throne where now that father sits,
his line still occupying it three hundred years
and more, although their roles will change.
No mean achievement for an unconsidered chit.

Lyn Moir

Elizabeth of Bohemia (1596–1662)

Praemunire

This foul cell curls my fingers into fists.
Cold penetrates my bones, and my eyes sting
from the smoke of guttering candles;
but nothing shall stay my hand as I pen
my pamphlet *Women's Speaking Justified*;
I will not rest until it is finished.

Nor while we are wrongfully denied
the liberty to worship as we choose.
Despised, imprisoned, tortured, our Friends
are cruelly abused, but though they are
beaten to swear an oath of allegiance,
they will not weaken and nor shall I.

These impregnable walls are breached by rain;
it drips onto the covers of my cot.
Sickness and disease are rife, and I pray
that I may survive long enough to see
my petition approved at last, and win
my appeal to return to Swarthmoor.

With God's good grace we may still be freed
to lead our lives as they were before –
no oath, no tithes, but still our meetings, for
as long as the Lord blesses me with a home,
I shall worship him in it
and no man, not even the King, shall stop me.

Barbara Hickson

Margaret Fell (1614–1702)

27

Getting Warmer

Science is of no country and of no sex.
Professor Joseph Henry, presenting Eunice Foote's experiment to the American
Association for the Advancement of Science, 23 August 1856

Seneca Falls, August 1856

Light washes me. The sun shouts
through the conservatory windows.
It has been dry weather. The garden beyond
wears its late-summer dress, green muslin
bravely splashed with orange and scarlet.
I hear the children calling to each other
like birds. In the angle of the open roof-pane,
a spider watches me from her web.

A fly buzzing. Sweat on my back.
Sleeves rolled above the elbow, collar
unbuttoned. This great skirt a nuisance.
I could work easier in my petticoats,
but I am not quite alone,
and my laboratory – flowerpots stacked
in one corner, rakes and spades and trowels in another –
is a glasshouse.

On the window-bench, the cylinders have stood in full sunlight.
Side by side, the mercuries rose, in their different atmospheres.
But not at the same pace. The rightmost cylinder,
containing carbonic acid – how much hotter it has become
than its bench-fellow filled only with moist air!
There is something important here. I know it.
I feel it, like the prickle of heat at my nape,
like my heartbeat. Something so simple it must be true.

In the cylinder, the carbonic acid absorbs heat.
And around the world, in the atmosphere we breathe,
is it the same? In the far past, I've read, Earth's air
was once richer in that gas. Might the world have been warmer
then? Might the gas itself be the cause?
And if in the past, why not again, in the future?

When I report on this, in three days' time,
I wonder if they will listen.

London, August 2026

Forty-one degrees. Only ten years ago
it would have been called a heatwave.
Not now. Now it's normal.
I am faint with the heat. The city is sticky with it.
We breathe soup. Garbage in the streets. Flies buzzing.
Sweat on my back. Walking to the library's an effort.
In Tasmania, in California, in Siberia, the land burns

because the world is warming. And Eunice was right.
But they did not listen. They listened, three years later,
to John Tyndall, at the Royal Society. Not to her.
Wrong sex, wrong time, wrong country,
wrong circles of acquaintance.
But Eunice was right, and now we all know it.

Mandy Macdonald

Eunice Newton Foote (1819–1888)

Do Not Allow

I slalomed, not too fast at first
    down the surfaces,
        in the box room they called my lab
from right to left and back again, squinting
    at the image; the dark shapes –
        tantalising. I tasted sweat – salty, stinging my eyes
as I inched down the twisting slope,
    gaining speed where the loop would
        double-back on itself, its two sugar-phosphate
backbones like the rails of a spiral staircase
    with guanine and cytosine, forming the steps. Somewhere
        the rails must come apart, each base seek
to mate with its complement – so two staircases are formed,
    the new identical to the old: the mark
        of the double helix: DNA;
but not for me, not then.

    Adonai,
        do not allow me to become a cliché;
           the feminist icon of molecular biology,
               but let it be known that with freedom
           from the patriarchal prison in sight, I dared to
    mock the death of the helix (double) DNA.

Gauche Watson, slick Crick
    stole the limelight I lit for them –
        their terrible Rosy Franklin who might have been
attractive if she took off her glasses –
    did something
        with her hair – I knew what they thought
before they put it in writing. Now my father
    can give thanks to his Eternal God –
        not mine – who kept him alive, sustained him,
enabled him to see me almost reach this
    season of triumph, although, my work
        was incomplete before he could
say kaddish for me. There is not, I think
    a Hebrew blessing for almost.

Wendy Klein

Rosalind Franklin (1920–1958)

What Is Life...?

Dear heart
standing so tall
and glowing
your smile dauntless
your divine voice
drawing the full pools
through shining sluices
of sound

I feel a little presumptuous
addressing you like this –
only - you always were
the whole world's
darling Kathleen
and the pools still brim
for you

Joy Howard

Kathleen Ferrier (1912–1953)

A Passionate Heart

'I want to be more than my verses – I want to be this person who once lived here'.

In Dobell's portrait, she is ninety-one, serene,
silver-haired, lace at her neck.
She plays it regally in voluminous black –

a doyenne, about to give the speech of her life,
wistful eyes glinting over a set mouth – her gloved hands
belie her spread of work still to be done.

She has the solidity of sculpture – Dame Mary Gilmore,
legend-making, seeing her city change,
as it has changed her.

She holds the arms of her chair as if to steady herself,
eyes staring ahead, protective of her nine decades:
politics, poetry.

Words burn in her palm. Though
dressed like a queen, she has known
a life of scrubbing floors, scrubbing words...

Her life was words – shone as a torch lighting up.
Paraguay, back to Australia. From one new world
to another, her search for justice, to renew.

Katherine Gallagher

Mary Gilmore (1864–1962)

32

Spartan Woman

Even twenty-seven centuries later, it seems neat to use
as a bookmark in a history of Helen, a geranium petal.

The flower bought for its beauty: blood-red, velvety,
radiant as bougainvillea hedges in Mediterranean light.

We all know Helen: the enchanting blonde
who's a helpless pawn in the game of men's lusts;

or the upright wife shockingly overcome
with desire for her resolute seducer.

Her influence ripples on. Some girls today
take photos of themselves, then use technology

to iron out their imperfections
and post their improved image on-line to woo lovers

who feel cheated when they meet them in the flesh.
But there's surgery for that – now every woman

if she undergoes enough procedures
can be as irresistible as Helen.

Attracted by the geranium on my table, a wasp
has landed on my arm. It's beautiful.

Frances Nagle

Helen of Troy (?)

An Astronomer's CV

Knitted quantities of cotton stockings.
Slaved as mother's laundry maid and scullion.
Endured smallpox and typhus.
Was rescued by William and taken to England.
Sang solo in the *Messiah*.
Dressed in layers of woollen petticoats.
Spent long winter nights watching the stars.
Sat in a booth under William's forty-foot telescope
With celestial clocks, a lamp, a journal
And a flask of coffee. Kept an observation record.
When William was too busy to stop and eat
Fed him by hand, like a mother bird her fledgling.
Polished the brass of the telescope.
Was given her own. Slept little.
Went to bed at dawn. Wrote home that she was
'Minding the heavens' and 'sweeping the sky'.
Played hostess to troops of wise men. Danced
Through the tube of the largest telescope.
Discovered seven new comets. Rode
On horseback to Greenwich to announce
The seventh's arrival. Moved out of the house
When William married. Minded his son.
Minded. Kept *A Book of Work Done*.

Diana Hendry

Caroline Herschel (1750–1848)

Lux Vivens

No need of icons, illuminated
missals, the flow of multi-coloured
frescoes over convent walls,

for the candle's shifting glance
to paint indigo shadows on
the stone, she had her own

library of images, kaleidoscope,
magic lantern, codex, wunder-
kammer, prisoner's cinema, screen.

She said her visions came
from God but complained they
split her head, her eyes were

blinded by the light
that was like no light seen
on earth, the living light

that permeates all life, a light
divine, the fire of God, His
flame that kindled in the nun

the *lux vivens*: the splendour
of the sun, the ways of God revealed
in visions painted one after one

in dragon's blood, lapis-lazuli,
malachite, saffron, gold. She left us
mere glimmers of a light that can't

be depicted nor described, like
the phosphorescent gleams a swimmer leaves
on the dark Ionian sea, when she dives.

Gabriel Griffin

Hildegard of Bingen (1098–1179)

35

Objets Sacrés

Five swords
four plain, one of great artistry
recovered from Sainte-Catherine-de-Fierbois
on your instructions. You once smote a whore
on the back with it and the king was displeased:
'The sword is anointed as you are.'

A white harness
each piece perfectly moulded to your body,
the greaves, knee plates, hauberk and cuirass,
spaulders and the gauntlets,
the polished breastplate fitted with an arret de cuirasse.
A gambeson of horsehair.

The spurs you never required.

Two silver rings.
One from your mother inscribed Jesu Maria.
Both confiscated by the English
and most likely melted down.

A white embroidered banner of boucassin
fringed with silk,
worked by careful women in Tours
who kissed every stitch.

Unpicked.

A wooden spoon and bowl you scraped
food from, frugally, burned on the pyre
with your shoes.

The bascinet you wore into battle,
behind glass in a museum in New York City.

Dented.

The plain cross in your tent
though you needed no reminding of God
who lived in the light of the fire
that so happily consumed you.

Julie-ann Rowell

Jeanne d'Arc (c 1412–1431)

Gardening Boots

after Sir William Nicholson (1920)

Waiting here in black,
well worn,
their last, most comfortable shape –
curves of her second skin –
as familiar with the genius of the place
as the genius herself,
every corner of Munstead Wood
trodden,
planted,
prodded into life.

Out in the cold,
until the last light and frosty air
settled on her garden,
rooks long since gathering;
reluctantly,
she would turn,
return to the warmth of home,

boots left outside
soil-encrusted,
laces askew,

tongues
drooping
into the void

waiting
to be filled.

Barbara Dordi

Gertrude Jekyll (1843–1932)

The More Famous

Have you got a brother, Puss?
Do you sometimes wish you hadn't?
Augustus Pussycat. A fine name.
Do you like it when I stroke you like that?
I envy you your simple life:
fish, milk, sleep, paw-washing.

Nothing makes me purr like painting
my studio or women sideways on
or, sometimes, Puss, the likes of you.
You're very handsome, did I tell you that?
I told Monsieur Rodin he was beautiful
but he just went on sculpting *The Kiss*.

Now he's returning my notes,
cutting me in the street.

She should have christened me Augusta
after herself. Augusta John.
That would have made them sit up.

People of the future, can you hear me?
Is it true they call Augustus
'brother of the more famous Gwen?'

Carole Bromley

Gwen John (1876–1939)

The Blue House

My pelvis is a palette
              on which night
is mixing day's colours.

Yellow is iodine,
white a sugar skull
with my name on its forehead.
Nothing is black, really *nothing*.

There are no shadows in this house,
only monkeys and parrots,
only Granizo my pet fawn –
              he is my right foot.

But over there, in the corner,
is my red boot with bells,
to cover my prosthesis.

And time?
              What colour is time?
Time is a green bus where I lie at an angle,
pierced by a purple pole.

Time is my orange womb, skewered
on a cobalt trolley.

And this is how I started painting.
Time stretched out its spectrum
and screeched its brakes.

Pascale Petit

Frida Kahlo (1907–1954)

Into the Flow

From where you stand you watch my faltering feet
brush tentative across each step, establishing
they don't come yet, the obstacles that wait
to trip me into fright.
You pity now my yearning hand that palpitates
the empty air, and dare to mutter in the presence
of my lost and open face that I don't walk
as surely as I might.
I say to you who travel past me through your world of sight
if you had known the dark from which I came
then you would call this light.

Across your talk you hear my flattened tones
risked in the room unmonitored by ear,
The modulation tutored by slow patience,
I aware I may give out some strange
unearthly noise, and all but I
will know when I am doing wrong.
I may be an intrusion in your world of sound
but there is one who crossed the torrents of my silences
and she would call this song.

On to my hand the flow, the chill flow,
into the flow she guided my hand, over and again,
patterning with her fingers on my palm
in letters – water, water.
Around my wild arms her strong arms,
into the flow she pushed my wondering hand,
on to my palm she patterned over and again
in letters – water, water.
Into my hand the flow,
out of her hand the patterns
until my sense woke, the darkness broke,
A shell cracked, split and fell back,
until the thirst rose, and her hand spoke,
into the flow she pushed my hand,
until the tide burst
and there was water.

Melanie Penycate

Helen Keller (1880–1968)

41

Cotton Flower

While Kashmir's jade valleys were torn apart,
lotuses blossomed in each sapphire lake.
Our saints and scriptures praise their sacred heart,
but I love cotton blooms for your dear sake.

Like cotton's spread, your moving yarn has grown.
You danced sky-clad, though cotton clothes the globe.
The cotton flower's journey mapped your own:
the tussle to transform from bud to robe.

In the combing and cleaning by ginner
and carder, the turning of each fine strand
of gossamer by a master spinner –
Lalla, you felt the Guru's guiding hand.

Like the weaver who stretched yarn on his loom,
the washer-man who scrubbed cloth with soap,
the tailor who cut what was once a bloom,
you were changed by suffering, faith and hope.

Kashmir's jade valleys still cry out in pain,
but your words yet echo in her hillsides
like cotton flowers that blow from the plain.
Lalla, everyone's darling and our pride.

Debjani Chatterjee

Lalleshwari (1320–1392)

Autoportrait

The rules don't apply,
not on this road, not in this life.

Maria Górska was left in the dust,
the wrong marque for this cougar,
the sleek mink who slipped through
countries, conformity,
boundaries, bedrooms,
lovers and husbands.

Tamara was born by her design
and reborn to sell in changing fashions,
adapting her machined, seductive curves,
advancing light and bright bold colours,
always racing, racing to luxury and fame.

She drives fast with one glove
light on the wheel,
scorning the slow,
cutting corners,
exultant across eight decades,
until her ashes soar over
the volcano's crimson lips.

Marka Rifat

Tamara de Lempicka (1898–1980)

Strong Boots

Dress suitably in short skirts and strong boots, leave your jewels in the bank and buy a revolver. Fashion advice to suffragettes and other political activists

let me tell you a story

let me tell you of an Irish patriot
grew up in Lissadell
knew WB and Maude G and the rest
a painter actor activist
married a Count from Ukraine

let me tell you about the Easter Rising
armed and determined
she joined up and joined in
was barricaded in St Stephen's Green for six days
ceased fire only for the park keeper to feed the ducks

let me tell you about gaol
at least four times they locked her up
jeered as she and seventy men were paraded
through the streets to Dublin Castle
death sentence commuted to life
'because of her sex'
she wished they'd had the decency to shoot her

let me tell you about the politician
the first woman elected to Westminster
(not taken up of course)
then elected to the Dáil
but died just five weeks later
in the poor ward
her jewels long given away

let me tell you she died too young

Jennifer Russell

Constance Gore-Booth Markievicz (1868–1927)

At St Kilda's

Nr. Melbourne, Australia

In a café called Monroe's she's everywhere.
Arms up, hands down, blown baby hair.
Her wide gaze stares from all the walls.
And in that stepped-up Warhol way, one image
in the strapless dress, follows you upstairs.

Even in the Ladies, she is innocent
through articulate graffiti. Below, etched
in black and white, she's emerging
from a limousine in ermine, bewildered
on a subway train, rapt in Arthur Miller glasses.

Or in that hooded wrap, white towelling
and only thigh-high with the breakers foaming.
Behind a pillar near the bar, early Norma Jean,
ship's prow pose, she lies uncomfortably, open-mouthed.
Her signature now, a spider scrawl,
thick ink, like icing on a cake. But black.

Outside, scorching sunlight and a grating
in the pavement. Young Monroes, (and there are many)
have sweet flesh like hers. But skirts too short to swirl,
in memory of that smiling Marilyn,
one leg turned inwards, high-heeled, peep-toed,
white-pleated billowing; frilled out to the wind.

Josie Walsh

Marilyn Monroe (1926–1962)

Interiors

Young, chaperoned by her mother,
Berthe chases light, sunshine, wind,
experiments with bold brushstrokes,
is, with the other Imressionists,
equally reviled by reviewers as mad.
Reckoned by male artists
as an equal talent,
she paints *In the Wheatfield*,
The Old Track to Auvers,
as no one had ever seen them.

Married, she scandalises society
by continuing to paint,
her subjects now domestic.
Her girls and women part curtains,
gaze from balconies, lean on railings,
lounge on verandas,
looking out while the world goes by
beyond them.
But we gain the incomparable
Le Berceau, her distillation
of what it means to be a mother,
then, always.

The Impressionists now feted,
she exhibits but sells little,
though a critic wrote in *Le Temps*,
'There is only one Impressionist in the group
and that is Berthe Morisot.'
When the French State came to describe her
on her death certificate it wrote
'No profession'.

Jo Peters

Berthe Morisot (1841–1895)

October 2020

Where are you now, Florence,
with your no-nonsense care,
making do, while legions bled,
sweated, defecated, wept?

How did you cope
with nurses to train, nuns to instruct,
when every moment dripped
with howls of pain, the stench of open sores?

How could you balance numbers
when ten times more soldiers
were taken by typhus, typhoid, cholera, dysentery
than battle wounds?

Your wards were overcrowded,
not antisocially distanced.
You fretted over defective sewers, poor ventilation,
not a lack of hand sanitiser.

You slashed the death rate
without PPE, track and trace, herd immunity,
lockdown, following the science,
masks for all, apps and latex gloves.

Where will your spirit be
when the lamp, that hovers
over three thousand beds that bear your name,
gutters out?

Alison Chisholm

Florence Nightingale (1820–1910)

A Quiet Rebel

And didn't she do a thousand things
after The Bus? wasn't she there
at the March on Washington when
the men spoke out, and the women sang

and didn't she weep with her Mama
when Martin Luther King Jnr,
the man who taught her that
non-violence is not a weakness, was shot

and didn't she read of the death of her friend,
Fannie Lou Hamer – another tired woman,
tired of all this beating, all this hate
sick and tired of being sick and tired

and didn't she tell us of prisoners,
and case after case of wrongfully accused,
who celebrated Joann Little's release,
but died before Gary Tyler's freedom

and didn't she, who never stopped believing,
know that it took more than legislation
to change things, and that her life was so much more
than keeping her seat that one time on a bus?

Eleanor J Vale

Rosa Parks (1913–2005)

48

Prima Ballerina

Since childhood she was always intense, frail,
highly strung, full of Slavic contradictions,
talked and moved fast, looked wistful,
born to sorrow, while dignity and elegance hid
stamina and discipline. She was known for her
delicacy, grace and weightless movement
on her feather-like flight across the stage.
She soared with precision, showed oriental
languor and melancholy, conveyed every nuance
of passion in pirouette, glissade, fouetté.

Dancing, she shimmered, gleamed, drifted,
floated, trembled, lived and breathed her art.
At night in the wings she crossed herself.
She wandered the world, seasick, undernourished,
living on herring and gingerbread. She performed
in a Mexican bullring. In China could complete
thirty-seven turns on the back of a moving elephant.
She practised all day to make people forget
their sad, hard lives. In her chosen dances
death was a recurring theme. She coughed and said,
'I have not yet had time to rest'.

Jenny Morris

Anna Pavlova (1881–1931)

Falling Silent

From the heart of the old wood
    a hundred birds flew
        singing of streams   skies   dawn –
passion taking flight
    as if nothing else was so alive
        as if they were drunk on something wonderful
like love was all here.

And my father   eyes closed   head tilted
    to the evening radio
        my mother stopping everything
to steal a moment of the Delius Cello Concerto
telling me
        this sound is blood   making everything possible.

And I too young to know why
    one beautiful October day my mother cried
        and cried for *the golden girl*
in her bluebell-blue silk dress playing as if she'd invented music
    running with nature   wild   trusting   imagining
        everyone was like her   that this
            could go on forever.

Kerry Darbishire

Jaqueline du Pré (1945–1987)

50

The Mystic and the Thief

I imagine her here, in some quantum future,
her summers in hedgerows, winters in a corrugated shed
where she plays cards with God, who cheats, of course,

or plaits her hair, uncombed for centuries. She asks him
for a love that is out of this world and he replies
her soul is too old for trinkets. She does not lament

the garden of Eden, that sweet homeland between
the Tigris and Euphrates, once heavy with angels,
but prays for the whole earth to wake from pain,

to forgo its journeys to the black box of the Kaaba,
the crosses and synagogues, asanas of yoga,
all that greed for the milk and honey of heaven.

Nor does she grieve at the loss of her beauty,
but welcomes the truth of what she will become,
lets herself be scoured by that longing for union

when she will take between her hands the much-loved
face on which the seven worlds are written, marry
that silence whose love leaves all words behind.

I think of her most when it's hot at night and I open
the window, remember the thief who climbed
over the sill into her sparse bedroom. Would I do

what she did? Recognise the smell of ocean,
know him as another creature out of water,
hair braided with kelp and badderlocks?

And, before he can snatch my blanket, fold
every piece of bedding, each last cotton sheet,
and hand them to him like a dowry?

Rosie Jackson

Rabia of Basra (c 714–801)

51

Giving Her Heart

We have no snow upon snow this year,
Just wind and rain and a blackened river.
In your day Midwinter was bleaker,
before power stations and cars.
Yet your childhood sounds warmer than ours.
A gaiety of visiting émigrés heated your parlour;
you talked poetry with Grandfather Polidori,
lent your face to brother Dante's art. No wonder
your head hummed with singing birds and sprites.

I would not change with you, even so.
Only men could gain brotherhood of arts then,
however Pre-Raphaelite.
You were taught to come second, posed as virgin
until you could play no other part.
Faith knitted you a thin comforter and you did your duty,
cared for mother and aunts, hid your body in bombazine.
By the time cancer beat you, you must have wondered
if life was worth your song.

A hundred years on, two galleries are full of you.
Your features cover their walls.
As I walk into a London Winter, my mind
sings your rhythms, your carols lift my soul.
Despite our differering times, we share so much:
a woman's conscience, mother, aunts...
too little time for creation.
Suddenly, in my head, I am writing again.
After eight months' silence words bang at my brain.

Watching Christmas lights plait along the river,
I thank you, Christina. Your bleak Midwinter
has thawed my own.

Pauline Kirk

Christina Rossetti (1830–1894)

Tinder and Flint

(A letter to Virginia Woolf)

Pale as an asphodel, your face still haunts me,
and I am glad. I have you to myself now,
imprisoned here in my tower, in my mind.

Each day I spiral up to greet you.
Your lips betray the suggestion of a smile,
your eyes, as always, never quite meet mine.

The wind keeps tapping on my window,
muttering to itself as it rattles at my door.
It lifts the edges of my pages as I try to write,
and throws stony raindrops up against the glass.

My winter garden has become a ghost of itself.
Roses undress, perennials play dead,
the trees cast long cadaverous shadows.

But summer's heat still lingers in the bricks, warm
memories of dense Ispahan and Maiden's Blush, mingling
their heady scent in the hush of velvet moth-trembling dusks.

What a searing plume it was, sparking off such storms
– tinder and flint, tinder and flint –
garnering rich yields of inspiration, gifting us words.

But some storms fail to clear the air, instead they lay waste.
One autumn, you heard the leaves' soft whisper
become an urgent rasp, and in the small talk of the river
a persistent invitation, offered through the darkness

of your shortening days. And then the vernal waves prevailed.
The hours stopped, the years ended.
                                    Our moment had passed.

Mary Anne Smith

Vita Sackville-West (1892–1962)

Free Fall

Consider Sappho shivering in her summer dress.
Bird boned in the glint of the moon's thin blade,
she walks ahead on the cliff path of tender grass.
Like you she loved pomegranate trees, oleanders made
thick with flowers, watched clouds pass like camels
padding the bare hills of Eressos with cushioned feet.

Despite slander and the warp of time, think well
of her, for her bold, gentle heart, poems to blast
hypocrisy, her belief in love's immortality – wings,
clipped never silenced the lark. I take your arm, casually,
your words like compass needles reverberate and sing
through rock, earth's chalk skin, the tumbling sea.
Even the grass grows pale when we dare look down.
You pull back as though you had always known.

Sue Davies

Sappho (c 600 BC)

Sometimes women are asking questions

in the bathtub with gertrude stein Angelica Freitas (trans Hilary Kaplan)

I see you, Gertrude, stepping out on rue de Fleurus,
with Alice B, in hats, long coats buttoned up and
that great big white little dog – simple through
complication. Lucky for him he had a pedigree
since the Nazis forbade feeding any other dogs.
My daughter would say you're no longer relevant.
I'd cringe too if you spoke to the men ignoring
our wives. But look at the huge splash you make
sliding about in a Brazilian poet's bathtub just
to grab her rubber duck. You like the view but turn
your broad back on it. What are you gazing at
beyond Oakland, Paris, Tangier? Ever sticking out
dear sore thumb, mustard pot in a coal scuttle.
What does it take to get by and who will hide us?

Maria Jastrezębska

Gertrude Stein (1874–1946)

Thoughts on the Education of Daughters

after the book of the same name

In these pages
is where I will always be,
not in the valleys'
soft waters of custom
but on mountain peaks,
words frozen as they left me.

You may falter on black ice
hidden under newest snow,
but if you will reach me,
follow the flag-marked track.
Climb carefully, take your time;
the air is thin here.

Barbara Dordi

Mary Wollstonecraft (1759–1797)

Dream

I'm at the window
watching the road
travelling in the wrong direction.

I see nothing bright or specific
just a continuous blankness
my duty must resolve

with a new nib,
to enclose everything
until the paper wears thin.

Behind me, my diaries
stacked to a height
of considerable risk,

every outing and encounter
contained, everything
I need never say again

on the point of collapse.
It's all done. Each trumped
argument, everything complete.

The river, losing its chalky blue light
as soon as someone slips in.

Gill Horitz

Virginia Woolf (1882–1941)

Notes

One of the most significant Russian poets of the 20th century, **Anna Akhmatova**'s work was condemned and censored by Stalinist authorities, but she chose not to emigrate and remained in the Soviet Union, acting as witness to the events around her. She was shortlisted for the Nobel Prize in 1965.

Only the second woman to do so, French mountaineer **Henriette d'Angeville** climbed Europe's highest peak, Mont Blanc, in 1838. She continued to climb until the age of 65, scaling twenty-one more peaks as well as again summiting Mont Blanc.

The greatest French actress of the later 19th and early 20th centuries and one of the best-known figures in the history of the stage, **Sarah Bernhardt** was often the subject of controversy but remained beloved of her audiences. In 1960 she was given a Star on Hollywood's Walk of Fame.

Queen of England from 1533 to 1536 as the second wife of King Henry VIII, **Ann Boleyn** was executed for treason and other charges, likely to have been false. Her marriage to the king made her a key figure in the political and religious upheaval that marked the start of the English Reformation.

A French artist in a realist style, **Rosa Bonheur** was primarily a painter of animals but also a sculptor. She became the first female artist to be awarded the Legion of Honour in 1865 and, 30 years later, was the first woman ever to become an Officer of the Legion of Honour.

A much revered sixth century Irish abbess, **St Bridget of Kildare** was the founder of several communities of nuns. She shares an association with the spring season, fertility, and healing with Brigid, a goddess of pre-Christian Ireland. Her feast day on 1st February was originally the pagan festival of Imbolc, marking the beginning of Spring.

A British nurse working in Belgium during WW1, **Edith Cavell** is celebrated for saving the lives of soldiers from both sides without discrimination and in helping some 200 Allied soldiers escape from German-occupied Belgium. She was found guilty of treason by court-martial and executed by a German firing squad.

Polish and naturalized-French physicist and chemist, **Marie Curie** conducted pioneering research on radioactivity. She was the first woman to win a Nobel Prize, the first person to win two Nobel Prizes and the only person to win in multiple sciences.

A militant fighter for the suffragette cause, British activist **Emily Wilding Davison** was arrested on nine occasions, went on hunger strike seven times and was force fed on forty-nine occasions. She died after being hit by King George V's horse at the 1913 Derby when she walked onto the track during the race.

Celebrated in the media for her unconventional approach to charity work, **Diana, Princess of Wales** was also the subject of much controversy. However, her charisma and friendly approach endeared her to the public and following her death in a car crash in Paris the extent of public mourning was unprecedented.

American aviation pioneer **Amelia Earhart** was the first female aviator to fly solo across the Atlantic Ocean. During an attempt to make a circumnavigational flight of the globe, she and her navigator Fred Noonan disappeared over the central Pacific. No trace has ever been found.

Second child of James VI of Scotland, I of England and Anne of Denmark, **Elizabeth of Bohemia** had thirteen children, one of whom was mother of George I of Great Britain. Beautiful, high spirited and a fluent linguist, during the period of the Thirty Years War she was influential in promoting the Protestant cause in Europe.

A founding member of the Religious Society of Friends and one of the Valiant Sixty, **Margaret Fell** is considered to be the mother of Quakerism. She was committed to life imprisonment and forfeiture of her property in 1664.

British contralto **Kathleen Ferrier**, whose unpretentious warmth combined with her unique vocal qualities made her a much loved figure, achieved an international reputation as a stage, concert and recording artist prior to her untimely death. Her repertoire extended from folksong and popular ballads to major classical works.

In her experiments with heating gases in the sun **Eunice Foote**, an American amateur scientist, inventor and feminist, discovered and identified the greenhouse effect, but her prescient insights were overshadowed and remained unknown for over 150 years.

British chemist and X-ray crystallographer **Rosalind Franklin**'s work was central to the understanding of the molecular structures of DNA, RNA, viruses, coal, and graphite. Other scientists used it as evidence to support their DNA model and took credit for the discovery.

According to Greek legend **Helen of Troy**, also known as Helen of Sparta, was said to have been the most beautiful woman in the world and the cause of the Trojan War. Famously named as 'the face that launched a thousand ships' by Christopher Marlowe.

German-British astronomer, **Caroline Herschel** was the younger sister of astronomer William Herschel, with whom she worked throughout her career. Her most significant contributions to astronomy were the discoveries of several comets. She was the first woman to do so.

Also known as St Hildegard and the Sibyl of the Rhine, **Hildegard of Bingen** was a German Benedictine abbess, writer, composer, philosopher, Christian mystic, visionary, and polymath of the High Middle Ages.

A national heroine of France, **Jeanne d'Arc** an was a peasant girl who, believing that she was acting under divine guidance, led the French army in a momentous victory at Orléans that repulsed an English attempt to conquer France during the Hundred Years' War. She was later tried as a heretic and burned at the stake.

British horticulturist, garden designer, craftswoman, photographer, writer and artist, **Gertrude Jekyll** created over 400 gardens in the UK, Europe and the US. She has been described as a premier influence in garden design. Some of her gardens have now been faithfully restored and can be visited.

Welsh artist **Gwen John** worked in France for most of her career. Her paintings, mainly portraits of anonymous female sitters, are rendered in a range of closely related tones. Originally overshadowed by her brother Augustus, she is now the more highly regarded of the two.

A Mexican painter known for her many portraits, self-portraits, and works inspired by the nature and artifacts of Mexico, **Frida Kahlo** endured many struggles with illness and disability which she explored through her art. She became an icon of the post-revolutionary Chicano Movement.

American author **Helen Keller** was the first deaf-blind person to earn a Bachelor of Arts degree. A political activist, her lecture tours took her several times around the world. She co-founded the American Civil Liberties Union.

Polish artist **Tamara de Lempicka** became a celebrated portrait painter who spent her working life in France and the US. Best known for her Art Deco portraits of aristocrats and the wealthy, and for her stylized paintings of nudes, she was flamboyant and eccentric to the last. Her ashes were scattered on Popocatepetl.

Kashmir's most famous poet-saint **Lalleshwari** was revered by both Hindus and Muslims. Her mystical poems – vakhs – are among the earliest writing in Kashmiri and are still sung today. A well-known vakh compares her spiritual journey to that of the cotton flower, which endures many changes before it becomes someone's clothing.

Irish nationalist, suffragist and socialist politician **Countess Constance Markievicz**, was the first woman elected to the Westminster Parliament, and was elected Minister for Labour in the First Dáil, becoming the first female cabinet minister in Europe.

American actress **Marilyn Monroe**, comedienne, singer, and model became one of the world's most enduring iconic figures and is remembered both for her embodiment of the Hollywood sex symbol and her personal and professional struggles within the film industry.

French artist **Berthe Morisot** became a member of the circle of painters in Paris who became known as the Impressionists. She was married to the brother of Edouard Manet, and gave up working 'en plein air' because her husband disliked her windblown appearance.

British nurse, social reformer and statistician **Florence Nightingale** was the founder of modern nursing. Her experiences as a nurse during the Crimean War were foundational in her views about sanitation. During the global pandemic of 2020, several emergency hospitals were erected in her name.

An American activist in the civil rights movement best known for her pivotal role in the Montgomery bus boycott, **Rosa Parks** was also active in the Black Power movement and the support of political prisoners in the US. She has been called the first lady of civil rights and the mother of the freedom movement.

A Russian prima ballerina of the late 19th and the early 20th centuries, **Anna Pavlova** was a principal artist of the Imperial Russian Ballet and the Ballets Russes of Sergei Diaghilev. In 1911, Pavlova took a major step in her career by forming her own ballet company.

British cellist **Jacqueline du Pré** achieved enduring mainstream popularity at a young age. Despite her short career, she is regarded as one of the greatest cellists of all time. Her career was cut short by multiple sclerosis, which forced her to stop performing at the age of 28.

Sufi mystic and poet **Rabia of Basra** was the first woman to become a Muslim saint, and is one of the most famous and influential renunciant women of Islamic history. She left her family to live in the desert and became an inspirational ascetic, evoking many legends and tales while living a life of semi-seclusion.

Born into an artistically gifted English-Italian family, **Christina Rossetti** became one of the Victorian age's finest poets. The sister of Dante Gabriel, she has been associated with the Pre-Raphaelite movement. Many of her poems have been set to music, the best known probably being 'In the Bleak Midwinter'.

Aristocrat, author and garden designer **Vita Sackville-West** was a successful British novelist, poet, and journalist, as well as a prolific letter writer and diarist. On her writing desk in the tower at Sissinghurst she always kept a large framed photograph of Virginia Woolf.

In ancient times **Sappho** was revered as one of the greatest lyric poets, She lived on the island of Lesbos, and though probably bisexual is widely regarded as having being among the first to give expression to sexual love between women.

An advocate of the avant garde, American novelist, poet, playwright, and art collector **Gertrude Stein** was a central figure in the Parisian art world. She moved to Paris in 1903, and made France her home for the remainder of her life, which was shared with her partner Alice B Toklas.

British writer, philosopher, and advocate of women's rights **Mary Wollstonecraft** argued that women are not naturally inferior to men, but appear to be only because they lack education. Her unorthodox lifestyle inadvertently destroyed her reputation for almost a century, but she is now regarded as a founder of feminism.

Considered one of the most important modernist 20th century authors, British writer **Virginia Woolf** was a pioneer in the use of stream of consciousness as a narrative device. She is also known for her involvement in the influential intellectual circle known as the Bloomsbury Group and for her contribution to feminist ideas.

The Poets

Jean Atkin lives in Shropshire. Her latest collection is *How Time is in Fields* (IDP 2019). Her poetry has featured on BBC Radio 4 and is widely published. **Margaret Beston**, founder of *Roundel*, a Poetry Society Stanza, lives in Tonbridge. She has been widely published in magazines and anthologies, and has published two collections, *Long Reach River,* 2014 and *Timepiece,* 2019. **Sara Boyes** has two collections *Kite* (Stride, 1989*), Wild Flowers* (Stride, 1993) and a pamphlet *Black Flame,* (Hearing Eye, 2005). She's been an actor, a playwright and, for many years, a tutor in creative writing. **Carole Bromley** lives in York. Her fourth collection, *The Peregrine Falcons of York Minster,* was published in 2020 by Valley Press. **Moya Cannon** is an Irish poet with six published collections, the most recent being *Donegal Tarantella* (Carcanet Press, 2019). Her *Collected Poems* is due from Carcanet Press in 2021. **Debjani Chatterjee** is a Sheffield-based poet and counsellor. Her six poetry collections include *Namaskar: New & Selected Poems.* Honours include an MBE, an honorary doctorate and RSL and RLF fellowships. **Alison Chisholm** is a poetry tutor and adjudicator, and the author of twelve collections. She writes poetry columns for *Writing Magazine,* and textbooks on the craft of writing poetry. **Kerry Darbishire** lives in Cumbria. She has two poetry collections published by Indigo Dreams. Her poems appear in anthologies and magazines. Kerry is currently working on a third collection. **Sue Davies** lives in Hampshire. Her first collection *Blue Water Café* was published in 2014. A prize-winning poet, her second collection of poetry will be ready for publication in 2021. **Julia Deakin's** work is widely published and praised by leading UK poets. She lives in West Yorkshire and edits *Pennine Platform* magazine. **Barbara Dordi** edits *The French Literary Review*, a bilingual arts magazine published in colour. In France for 12 years, she published poetry and a biography: *Achille Laugé Neo-Impressionist 1861–1944.* **Elsa Fischer** has two pamphlets *Palmistry in Karachi* (Templar Poetry) and *Hourglass* (Grey Hen Press). Her poems have been anthologised and published in magazines including *The Rialto, erbacce, Mslexia,* and *ARTEMISpoetry.* **Katherine Gallagher** is widely-published in the UK and Australia, has six full collections, most recently *Acres of Light* (Arc Publications, 2016) and *Carnival-Edge: New & Selected* (Arc, 2010). **Gabriel Griffin** is the founder and organiser of *Poetry on the Lake* annual competition, festival and events on Lakes Orta & Maggiore, Italy. She has edited anthologies, won prizes and been placed in competitions. **Diana Hendry** has published seven poetry collections and many books for children. She's been a Royal Literary Fund Fellow, co-editor of *New Writing Scotland* and assistant editor of Mariscat Press. **Barbara Hickson's** poems have appeared in magazines, anthologies and on-line journals. She has a shared collection with Gabriel Griffin and Bev Morris, *Rugged Rocks, Running Rascals* (DragonSpawn Press, 2019). *Gill Horitz* has worked in the Arts for many years developing community theatre and creative projects, programming literature and running writing groups. Her first pamphlet is *All The Different Darknesses* (Cinammon, 2019). *Joy Howard* spends her days hiding away from Covid, accepting that her computer is now her best friend. The generosity of Grey Hen poets in sharing their work keeps her going. *Rosie Jackson* lives in Devon. Widely published, her most recent poetry collection is *Aloneness is a Many-Headed Bird* (Hedgehog Press, 2020), a collaboration with Dawn Gorman. *Maria Jastrzębska* is a poet, editor and translator. Her fourth collection was *The True Story of Cowboy Hat and Ingénue* (Cinnamon Press 2018). She co-edited *Queer in Brighton* (New Writing South, 2014). *Pauline Kirk* is a York poet, editor and novelist. Eleven poetry collections and three novels have been published under her own name, and four *DI Ambrose Mysteries* as PJ Quinn. *Wendy Klein* has published four collections *Cuba in the Blood* and *Anything in Turquoise* (Cinnamon Press); *Into the Blue: Selected Poems* (The High Window) and a pamphlet *Let Battle Commence* (Dempsey & Windle). *Mandy Macdonald* lives in Aberdeen. Her poems appear in several Grey Hen publications and in many anthologies and journals. Her debut pamphlet, *The temperature of blue*, was published by Blue Salt collective in 2020. *Lyn Moir* has published four collections, two with Arrowhead and two with Calder Wood Press. She still lives in St. Andrews, is still working on new collections. *Jenny Morris* has danced through life, but was never known for her feather-like flight. A down-to-earth person, she lives in Norfolk where wild geese fly. She has five collections and a pamphlet. *Frances Nagle* Poems in many magazines including *Poetry Review, London Magazine, The North, Poetry Wales*. Eternally grateful for music, poetry, the wonders of nature and the kindness of other humans. *Ise Pedler's* pamphlet *The Dogs That Chase Bicycle Wheels* won the 2015 Mslexia Pamphlet competition. Her first collection is due out with Seren in 2021. She works as a veterinary surgeon in Kendal. *Melanie Penycate* is a retired teacher living in a former Blacksmith's Forge in West Sussex. Her two collections are *Breaking the Arch* and *Feeding Humming Birds* and she chairs Chichester Stanza. *Jo Peters* has been published in magazines and anthologies and has had success in competitions. Her pamphlet *Play* and collection *like yellow like flying* are published by Half Moon Books. *Pascale Petit* has eight collections. *Tiger Girl* (Bloodaxe, 2020) is shortlisted for the Forward Prize. Her seventh, *Mama Amazonica*, won the inaugural Laurel Prize in 2020 and the RSL Ondaatje Prize in 2018. *Jennifer Russell* lives in County Cork, Ireland. She set up and co-runs Hungry Hill Writing, a writers' group which hosts two international poetry competitions a year. *Marka Rifat* writes poems, stories, articles and plays. This year, she has work in 16 anthologies in the UK and US. She lives in Aberdeenshire and battles with the elements. *Julie-ann Rowell* has four collections. Her poem 'Fata Morgana' from the most recent, *Exposure* (all about the islands of Orkney) was Highly Commended in the Forward Prize for Poetry 2020/2021. *Penelope Shuttle* lives in Cornwall. Her thirteenth collection, *Lyonesse,* appears from Bloodaxe Books, May 2021. A pamphlet *Father Lear (* Poetry Salzburg) was published in Summer 2020. *Mary Anne Smith* has been recognised in both national and international competitions, including first prizes in *O'Bheal Five Words* and *Sentinel Literary Quarterly.* Her work has also been widely published and broadcast. *Deborah Sloan* is a retired counsellor. Before the Covid times she ran poetry and writing workshops for people living with dementia, addiction or grief. She is working towards a collection. *Susan Utting* taught poetry and creative writing chiefly at Reading and Oxford Universities for more than twenty years. She is a Two Rivers poet and currently works freelance as tutor, workshop facilitator and performer. *Eleanor J Vale* lives in Suffolk. Her pamphlet *Think of Something Else* was published by the Garlic Press in 2016. She won the Grey Hen Poetry Competition in 2019. *Josie Walsh* lives in Wakefield. Initially published as Josie Kildea in *Beyond Bedlam* (Anvil Press, 1997), since retirement from teaching she has three collections published and has read on radio and at festivals.

Acknowledgments

JEAN ATKIN *How Time Is in Fields* (Indigo Dreams, 2019). SARA BOYES 'In St Martin's Fileds' on view in *Brussells at Dawn,* an installation created by Unity Arts at St Martin in the Fields, October 2015. CAROLE BROMLEY 'The More Famous' previously published as 'Gwen John' *The Peregrine Falcons of York Minster* (Valley Press, 2020). MOYA CANNON 'A Song at Imbolc' was commissioned by Galway 2020 and appeared in *The Irish Times.* DEBJANI CHATTERJEE 'Cotton Flower' previously published as'To Lalla' in *Spinning a Yarn: Weaving a Poem* (Sahitya Press 2018). KERRY DARBISHIRE 'Falling Silent' *Famous* (Dreich Themed Chapbook, Hybrid Press, 2020). GABRIEL GRIFFIN 'Lux Vivens' previously published as 'Hildegard, visions and inspiration' (Wyvern Works, 2012). DIANA HENDRY 'An Astronomer's CV' previously published as 'Caroline Herschel: Her CV' *The Watching Stair* (Worple Press, 2018). GILL HORITZ 'Dream' previously published as 'Woolf's Dream' *All The Different Darknesses* (Cinnamon Press, 2019). MARIA JASTRZĘBSKA 'Sometimes women are asking questions' *Noble Dissent* (Beautiful Dragons Collaborations, 2017). WENDY KLEIN 'Do Not Allow' *Pitshanger Poets Poetry Competition Anthology 2007.* PAULINE KIRK 'Giving Her Heart' previously published as 'To Christina Rossetti' *No Cure in Tears* (Aireings Publications, 1997) ,*Walking to Snailbeach: Selected and New Poems* (Redbeck Press, 2004) and in *A Taste of Pennine Poets* (Fighting Cock Press, 1995), *Aireings, Poetry Monash,* and *Poetry Church Collection.* LYN MOIR 'Miniature' previously published as 'Elizabeth of Bohemia' in *ARTEMISpoetry.* ILSE PEDLER 'Beyond Light' published in *Carillon.* MELANIE PENYCATE ' Into the Flow' previously published as 'Helen Keller' in *Weyfarers* and *Feeding Humming Birds* (Oversteps Books, 2009). PASCALE PETIT 'The Blue House' *The Wounded Deer* (Smith/Doorstop, 2005);*What the Water Gave Me* (Seren, 2010). JULIE-ANN ROWELL 'Objets Sacrés' previously published as 'Objets Sacrés:Jeanne d'Arc' *Voices in the Garden* (Lapwing Publications, 2017). PENELOP SHUTTLE 'Song Book' previously published as 'Ann Boleyn's Music Book' in *ARTEMISpoetry.* SUSAN UTTING 'Half the Human Race' *Half the Human Race: New & Selected Poems* (Two Rivers Press, 2017).

Joy Howard is the founder of Grey Hen Press, which specialises in publishing the work of older women poets. Her poems have featured in many anthologies and journals and can be found online at *poetry p f.* She has now edited seventeen Grey Hen Press anthologies, and published a collection of her own poems *Exit Moonshine* about her 'coming out' experiences in the 1980s. Her second collection, *Refurbishment*, was published by Ward Wood in 2011, and her most recent, *Foraging*, by Arachne Press in 2016.